ANIMALS AROUND THE WORLD

ALL ABOUT ASIAN ORANGUTANS

EZ READERS

Carol Kline

Creating Young Nonfiction Readers

EZ Readers lets children delve into nonfiction at beginning reading levels. Young readers are introduced to new concepts, facts, ideas, and vocabulary.

Tips for Reading Nonfiction with Beginning Readers

Talk about Nonfiction
Begin by explaining that nonfiction books give us information that is true. The book will be organized around a specific topic or idea, and we may learn new facts through reading.

Look at the Parts
Most nonfiction books have helpful features. Our *EZ Readers* include a Contents page, an index, and color photographs. Share the purpose of these features with your reader.

Contents
Located at the front of a book, the Contents displays a list of the big ideas within the book and where to find them.

Index
An index is an alphabetical list of topics and the page numbers where they are found.

Photos/Charts
A lot of information can be found by "reading" the charts and photos found within nonfiction text. Help your reader learn more about the different ways information can be displayed.

With a little help and guidance about reading nonfiction, you can feel good about introducing a young reader to the world of *EZ Readers* nonfiction books.

Mitchell Lane
PUBLISHERS

2001 SW 31st Avenue
Hallandale, FL 33009
www.mitchelllane.com

First Edition, 2020.

Author: Carol Kline
Designer: Ed Morgan
Editor: Sharon F. Doorasamy

Names/credits:
Title: All About Asian Orangutans / by Carol Kline
Description: Hallandale, FL :
Mitchell Lane Publishers, [2020]

Series: Animals Around the World
Library bound ISBN: 9781680204100
eBook ISBN: 9781680204117

EZ readers is an imprint of Mitchell Lane Publishers

Library of Congress Cataloging-in-Publication Data
Names: Kline, Carol, 1957- author.
Title: All about Asian orangutans / by Carol Kline.
Description: First edition. | Hallandale, FL : EZ Readers, an imprint of Mitchell Lane Publishers, 2020. | Series: Animals around the world-Asian animals | Includes bibliographical references and index.
Identifiers: LCCN 2018035298| ISBN 9781680204100 (library bound) | ISBN 9781680204117 (ebook)
Subjects: LCSH: Orangutans—Juvenile literature.
Classification: LCC QL737.P94 K55 2020 | DDC 599.88/3—dc23
LC record available at https://lccn.loc.gov/2018035298

Photo credits: Freepik.com, Shutterstock, mapchart.net

CONTENTS

Orangutans are gentle animals. They live in **rain forests**. Orangutan means "person of the forest."

The orangutan's hair is orange brown. They make **belching** noises to talk to each other.

Flanges are cheek-pads. They are large and flappy. Some adult male orangutans have flanges. Some do not. The flanges stick out from the side of the face.

A male orangutan grows to the size of a man. Females are half the size of males.

An orangutan's hands almost touch the ground when they stand. An orangutan's feet are like hands.

Orangutans love trees. They need trees to sleep and to find food.

Orangutans sleep in nests of leafy branches. They use leaves as umbrellas.

Orangutans eat fruit, leaves, and insects.

Young orangutans stay with their mothers until they are teens. Mothers teach their babies what to eat. They teach them where to find food too.

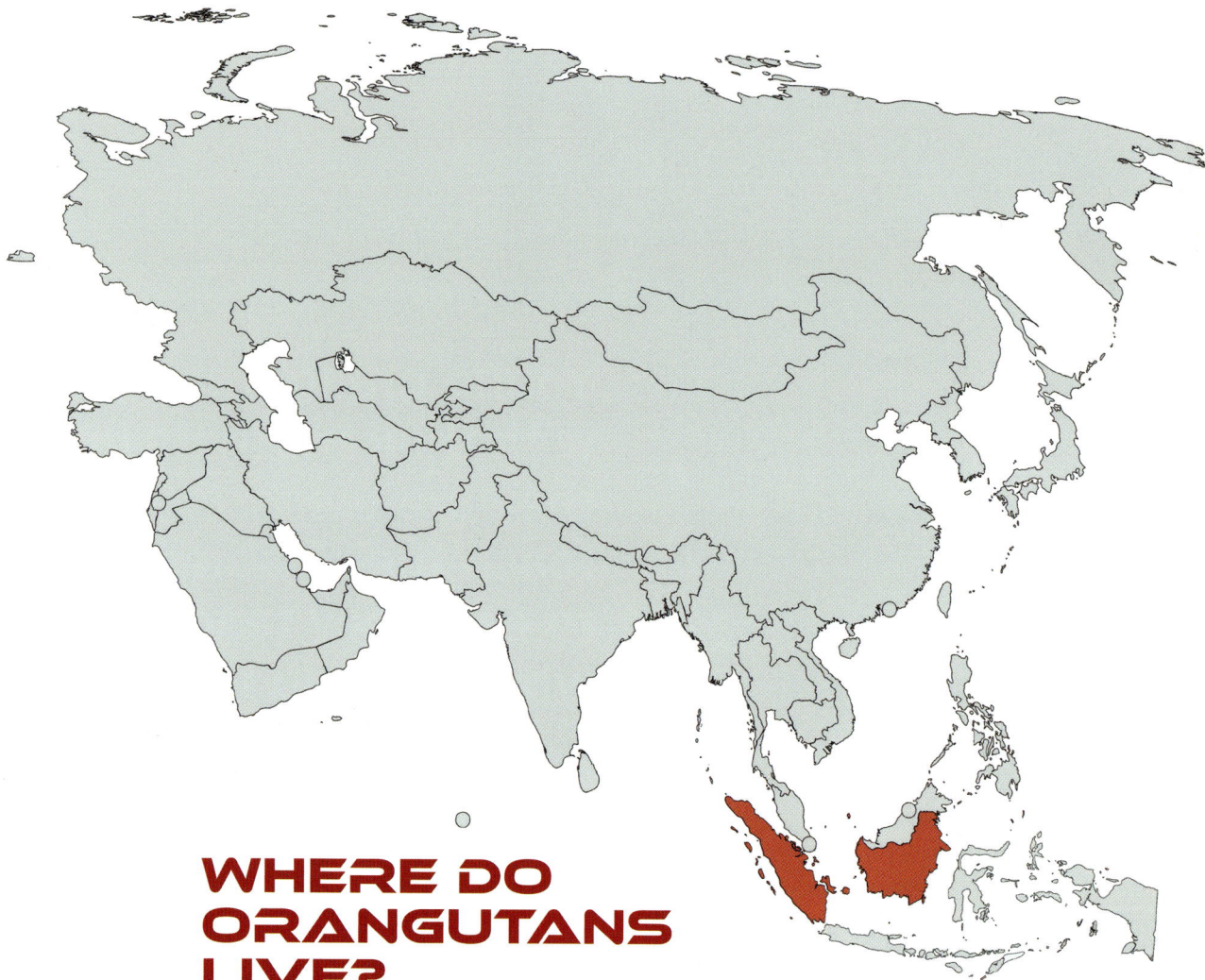

WHERE DO ORANGUTANS LIVE?

On the islands of Borneo and Sumatra in Indonesia. Indonesia is made up of many islands.

INTERESTING FACTS

- Orangutans can live to be 50 years old.

- Orangutans are very smart.

- An orangutan's feet are like hands because they can **grip** branches.

- It is easier for orangutans to climb and walk in trees than walk on the ground.

- Male orangutans make a noise called the "**long call**." It can be heard from a long distance.

- Orangutans are "gardeners" of the forest. They eat fruit and poop out the seeds. The seeds grow into more plants.

- Many trees are cut down in Indonesia. When the trees are cut down, it takes away the home of orangutans. This is a scary time for orangutans.

PARTS OF AN ORANGUTAN

Face
The face of an orangutan is black. Some males have a flange on either side of their face. Their eyes are small and black.

Arms
Orangutans have long arms that help them climb and move through trees.

Tail
Orangutans do not have a tail.

Fur
The fur of an orangutan is reddish or orange brown.

Hands and Feet
An orangutan has five fingers and toes on its hands and feet.

GLOSSARY

belch
To burp; let air from your stomach in a noisy way

flanges
An edge that sticks out on both sides of the orangutan's face

grip
To grab or hold (something) tightly

long call
Roars and groans that male orangutans make

rain forest
Forests in warm climates with tall trees and lots of rain

FURTHER READING

Eszterhas, Suzi. *Orangutan*. London: Frances Lincoln Childrens Books, 2013.

Kueffner, Sue. *Orangutans*. Pleasantville, NY: Gareth Stevens, 2009.

Underwood, Deborah. *Watching orangutans in Asia*. Chicago, IL Heinemann Library, 2006.

ON THE INTERNET

To hear sounds that an orangutan makes, visit this site:
https://wildambience.com/wildlife-sounds/orangutan/

To see pictures of the male's orangutan face flanges:
http://www.arkinspace.com/2014/08/the-mystery-of-orangutan-flange.html

INDEX